Italic

HANDWRITING SERIES

Third Edition

BOOK G

by

Barbara Getty and Inga Dubay

Continuing Education Press
Portland State University
Portland, Oregon

ITALIC HANDWRITING SERIES

BOOK A ▪ Basic Italic
14 mm body height

BOOK B ▪ Basic Italic
11 mm, 9 mm

BOOK C ▪ Basic Italic
9 mm, 6 mm   Introduction to Cursive Italic

BOOK D ▪ Cursive Italic
6 mm, 5 mm   including Basic Italic

BOOK E ▪ Cursive Italic
6 mm, 5 mm, 4 mm   including Basic Italic

BOOK F ▪ Cursive Italic
6 mm, 5 mm, 4 mm   including Basic Italic

BOOK G ▪ Cursive Italic
5 mm, 4 mm   including Basic Italic

INSTRUCTION MANUAL

THIRD EDITION

Copyright 1994 by Barbara M. Getty and Inga S. Dubay

ISBN 0-87678-098-2

06 05 04 03 02 01 00 99
15 14 13 12 11 10 09 08 07 06 05

Published and distributed by
CONTINUING EDUCATION PRESS
PORTLAND STATE UNIVERSITY
P.O. BOX 1394 ▪ PORTLAND, OREGON 97207

Printed in the United States of America

Printed with soy ink ✪ on recycled paper

CONTENTS

BASIC & CURSIVE ITALIC ALPHABET

BASIC ITALIC

All letters written in one stroke unless otherwise indicated.

Aa Bb Cc Dd Ee Ff Gg

or A³   *or e²*

Hh Ii Jj Kk Ll Mm

or   *or*

Nn Oo Pp Qq Rr Ss Tt

or   *or*

Uu Vv Ww Xx Yy Zz

0 1 2 3 4 5 6 7 8 9

CURSIVE ITALIC

All letters written in one stroke unless otherwise indicated.

Aa Bb Cc Dd Ee Ff Gg

ana bnb cnc dnd ene fnf gng

or ene

Hh Ii Jj Kk Ll Mm

hnh ini jnj knk lnl mnm

Nn Oo Pp Qq Rr Ss Tt

nnn ono pnp qnq rnr sns tnt

or sns

Uu Vv Ww Xx Yy Zz

unu vnv wnw xnx yny znz

INTRODUCTION

This, the seventh of seven books in the *Italic Handwriting Series*, provides an introduction or review of basic and cursive italic. It is recommended for sixth grade and beyond, including adults.

Italic handwriting is a modern system based on sixteenth century letter forms that first developed in Italy and were later used in England and Europe. Italic provides the young person and the adult with letter shapes that are highly suited to a rapid and legible handwriting. Italic is also an art form when written as formal calligraphy. The word calligraphy, from the Greek *kalli* (beautiful) and *graphia* (writing) generally refers to letters carefully handwritten with a monoline or edged tool. Italic calligraphy is one type of formal hand lettering. Part 3, pages 41-47, provides an introduction to the edged pen.

Writing is a system of conventional signs, and at any particular point in time, those using the system must be able to recognize the symbols and what they signify. The history of written symbols through the ages presents a fascinating story, and the writing practice in this book incorporates a brief history of our writing heritage. In addition, the introduction of cursive capitals includes the historical development of each letter.

It is suggested that you read a line or more of writing, trace the model letters, then copy them in the space provided. Tracing provides an awareness of finger and hand movements which may improve manual ability. Descriptions of lowercase letters, capitals, joins and numerals are given, emphasizing strokes, shape, size, slope, spacing and self-assessment.

We write for different occasions. Formal writing includes very carefully written reports, term papers, business letters, applications, forms, maps, signs, posters, thank you notes, and so forth. Informal writing may include more rapidly written daily assignments, letters and notes to friends, rough drafts of poems, stories, etc. Fast writing may include very rapidly written lists of homework assignments, telephone messages, your own personal notes, grocery lists, etc. A series of timed writings is provided to help increase writing speed at all levels of writing (p. 38).

Writing process, stroke information, directions, notes, reminders, options, and assessments are included in the margins. Further letter and join descriptions and assessment questions are found in the INSTRUCTION MANUAL.

Assessment is the key to improvement. The self-assessment method used enables you to monitor your own progress. STEP 1: You are asked to LOOK at the writing and affirm what is the best. STEP 2: You are asked to PLAN what needs to be improved and how to accomplish this. STEP 3: You are then asked to put the plan into PRACTICE. This LOOK, PLAN, PRACTICE format provides self-assessment skills applicable to all learning situations.

The enjoyment of good handwriting is shared by both the writer and the reader. Handwriting is a lifelong skill—good handwriting is a lifelong joy!

Certainly
THE ART OF WRITING
is the most miraculous
of all things   CARLYLE
man has devised.

BASIC ITALIC HANDWRITING, pp 1-14

The history of writing is,
in a way,
the history
of the human race...
FREDERICK W. GOUDY

CURSIVE ITALIC-EDGED PEN, pp 41-46

Handwriting
is a system of movements
involving touch.
ALFRED FAIRBANK

CURSIVE ITALIC HANDWRITING, pp 15-40

CALLIGRAPHY
grasps the mind
and makes the writing
come alive
LLOYD J. REYNOLDS

ITALIC CALLIGRAPHY-EDGED PEN, pp 47, 49

REMINDERS

PENCIL HOLD

Use a soft lead pencil (#1 or #2) with an eraser. Hold the pencil with the thumb and index finger, resting on the middle finger. The upper part of the pencil rests near the large knuckle.

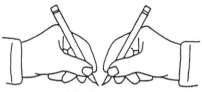

REGULAR HOLD

Hold the pencil firmly and lightly. AVOID pinching. To relax your hand, tap the index finger on the pencil three times.

Problem grips such as the 'thumb wrap' (thumb doesn't touch pencil) and the 'death grip' (very tight pencil hold) make it difficult to use the hand's small muscles. To relieve these problems, try this alternative pencil hold.

ALTERNATIVE HOLD

Place the pencil between the index finger and the middle finger. The pencil rests between the index and middle fingers by the large knuckles. Hold the pencil in the regular way at the tips of the fingers.

PAPER POSITION

LEFT-HANDED

If you are left-handed and write with the wrist below the line of writing, turn the paper clockwise so it is slanted to the right as illustrated. If you are left-handed and write with a "hook" with the wrist above the line of writing, turn the paper counter-clockwise so it is slanted to the left as illustrated. (Similar to the right-handed position)

RIGHT-HANDED

If you are right-handed turn the paper counter-clockwise so it is slanted to the left as illustrated.

POSTURE

Rest your feet flat on the floor and keep your back comfortably straight without slumping. Rest your forearms on the desk. Hold the workbook or paper with your non-writing hand so that the writing area is centered in front of you.

LINED PAPER CHOICES

The following choices for lined paper may be used when instructions say use lined paper for practice.

1. Lines 5mm body height on page 55 may be duplicated. These lines can also be used as guidelines under a sheet of unlined paper. Fasten with paper clips.

2. Lines 4 mm body height on page 56 may be duplicated. These lines can also be used as a line guide under a sheet of unlined paper. See INSTRUCTION MANUAL pp. 103-104 for lines with capital height.

3. Some school paper has a solid baseline and a dotted waistline. Use paper with a body height of 6mm ($\frac{1}{4}$") or 5mm ($\frac{3}{16}$").

4. Some school paper has only baselines. Use paper with lines 12mm ($\frac{1}{2}$") or 10mm ($\frac{3}{8}$") apart.

5. Use wide-ruled notebook paper with a space of about 9 mm ($\frac{3}{8}$") between lines, or college ruled notebook paper 7.5mm ($\frac{5}{16}$") between lines. Create your own waistline by lining up two sheets of notebook paper and shifting one down half a space. The faint line showing through will serve as a waistline.

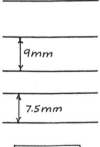

VOCABULARY

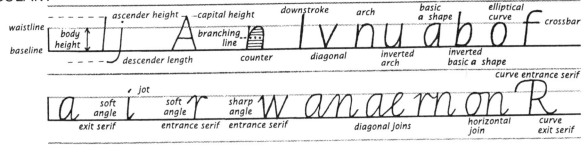

STROKES

Basic italic letters all start at the top and go down or over (horizontal), except **d** and **e**. (**d** starts at the waistline and **e** starts at the center of the body height.) Follow the direction of the arrow. Letters are written in one stroke unless otherwise indicated.

Trace the dotted line model, then copy model in space provided. If needed, trace solid line model.

LETTER ASSESSMENT

SHAPE:

Basic italic lowercase letters are divided into eight families according to shape. Basic italic capitals are divided into three width groups. Cursive italic lowercase joins are divided into eight join groups.

SIZE:

Letters are written with a consistent body height. Capitals, ascenders and descenders are written one and a half times the body height.

SLOPE:

The models are written with a 5° letter slope. A consistent slope is an important part of good handwriting. For individual slope choices see *Slope Guidelines*, page 40. See 5° slope page 54.

SPACING:

Letters are written close together within words. Joins are natural spacers in cursive italic; when lifts occur, keep letters close together. Spacing between words is the width of an **n** in basic and cursive italic. See *Spacing Guidelines*, page 40.

SPEED:

Write at a comfortable rate of speed. To increase the speed of writing use the *Timed Writing*, p 38. NOTE: See *OPTIONS*, page 39.

GOAL
To write legible, neat handwriting.

IMPROVEMENT
Assessment is the key to improving your handwriting. Follow this improvement method as you learn basic and cursive italic handwriting.

1. **LOOK** at your writing. Circle your best letter or join. Answer question about strokes, shape, size, spacing, or slope.

2. **PLAN** how to make your writing look more like the model. Pick the letter or join that needs work. Compare with the model.

3. **PRACTICE** the letter or join that needs work. Write on the lines provided and on lined paper.

★ Give yourself a star at the top of the page when you see you have made an improvement.

NOTE: See INSTRUCTION MANUAL, Assessment, pp. 54-68.

INFORMAL ASSESSMENT OF STUDENT PROGRESS

The main purpose of handwriting instruction is to promote legibility so that we can communicate with others and ourselves.

PRE-TEST Before you begin this book, write the following sentence in your everyday handwriting. Also write your name, address and today's date.

A quick brown fox jumps over the lazy dog.

Write the sentence.

1
2

Name

3

Address

4

City, State

5

Today's date

6

POST-TEST After you have completed this workbook, write the following sentence in cursive italic. Also write your name, address and today's date in cursive italic.

A quick brown fox jumps over the lazy dog.

Write the sentence.

7
8

Name

9

Address

10

City, State

11

Today's date

12

ASSESSMENT

SHAPE:	Each letter is similar to the models in the workbook.
SIZE:	Similar letters are the same height (for example: aec, dhk, gpy). Capital letters and lowercase letters with ascenders are the same height.
SLOPE:	Letters have a consistent letter slope (between 5° – 15°).
SPACING:	Letters within words are closely spaced. Spaces between words are the width of **n**.
SPEED:	Words are written fluently at a comfortable speed.

PART ONE

Basic Italic & Numerals

Lowercase
Capitals
Numerals
Writing Practice
Handwriting Tips

LOWERCASE FAMILIES *according to similar shapes*

i j l · k or k v w x z · h m n r · u y · a d g q · b p · o e c s · f t

FAMILY 1 2 3 4 5 6 7 8

These letters are presented at 9mm body height to help you focus on the letter shapes, tool hold, and hand movements before moving to a smaller, more natural letter size.

Write all letters in one stroke without lifting your writing tool unless otherwise indicated. Trace each letter, then write your own in the space provided. Take note of letter families and shapes as you practice.

FAMILY 1   *straight line downstroke (see vocabulary, p. vii)*

ascender height

waistline

branching line   9mm body height

baseline

descender length

FAMILY 2   *diagonal strokes*

k or R v w x z

cross x at branching line or slightly above

FAMILY 3   *arch*

branching line

h m n r

form arch by retracing downstroke back up to the branching line, then curve upward to the right

FAMILY 4   *inverted arch*

u y · u

WRITING PRACTICE · *keep letters close together within words*

kiwi k   hurry h

9mm

G

2

© 1994 Getty/Dubay

LOWERCASE FAMILIES, continued

FAMILY 5   *basic a shape*

begin horizontally

abrupt curve

a d g q

FAMILY 6   *inverted basic a shape*

FAMILY 7   *elliptical curve*

b p

o e

begin e at branching line   alternate 2-stroke e:

FAMILY 7, continued

FAMILY 8   *crossbar*

c s

f t

WRITING PRACTICE · *a pangram (a sentence containing all 26 letters of our alphabet)*

a quick brown fox

jumps over the lazy dog

9mm

Practice words and sentences on notebook paper, writing a space high. See pp. 48-49 for additional pangrams.

LOWERCASE FAMILIES *according to similar shapes (5mm body height)*

FAMILY 1 i j l · k *or* k v w x z · h m n r · u y · a d g q · b p · o e c s · f t
           1   2   3   4   5   6   7   8

All letters are written in one stroke with no pencil/pen lift unless otherwise indicated.

FAMILY 1
i j l

i i i i   j j j j   l l l l   RELAX

Trace & copy line above. Fill each line on the page.

Exhale on downstroke. This may help you write straight lines.

i   j   l

FAMILY 2
k v w x z

k k *or* k k   v v   w w   x x   z z

OPTION:

▢ 1
LOOK at your writing.

k   k   v   w   x   z

Trace and write: will will

FAMILY 3
h m n r

h h   m m   n n   r r

▢ 2
PLAN which letters need work. How will you make them look more like the models?

✏ Circle your best **m**.

h   m   n   r

mix mix   rim rim

FAMILY 4
u y

u u   y y

u   y

FAMILY 5
a d g q

a a a   d d d

▢ 3
PRACTICE on notebook paper the letters that need more work.

a   d

g g g   q q q

g   q

adding a

· PICTURE WRITING ·

As far as we know, about 28,000 B.C. people began painting pictures on the walls of the caves. Paintings of bison, rhinoceroses, horses and bulls have been found in Spain and France. Early paintings and drawings show animals in action—the beginning of storytelling.

FAMILY 6
b p

b b   p p   bumpy

b   p   b

5mm

SELF-ASSESSMENT: Do your letters slope in the same direction? bumpy

FAMILY 7
o e c s

Trace & copy
the line above.

o o o   e e e

OPTION:

or e e e

overlap stroke 2
over stroke 1

2-stroke e:
See page 24,
cursive join 3.

o   e   e

c c c   s s s

Circle your best o, e, c, & s.

c   s

· AMERICAN INDIAN SIGNS ·

bear tracks   mountains   rain clouds   tepee (tipi)   lightning

Before alphabets were developed,
many peoples of the world used pictures
to tell stories and to send messages and
instructions.

FAMILY 8
f t

f f f   t t t

t is a short letter!

f   t

ocean   tepee   clouds   mountains

ocean

PANGRAM   a quick brown fox jumps over the lazy dog

a

SHAPE
SLOPE
SPACING
STROKES

Trace & copy
this paragraph.

Lowercase italic is based on the elliptical*

shape. The letters slope slightly to the

The diagonal
lines at the right
are sloped 5° to
the right. Slope
your writing
0°–15° to the
right. Be
consistent.

right and are closely spaced. Twenty one

Tracing letters
gives you the
feel of the
letters and the
correct spacing
within and
between words.

of the letters are written in one stroke.

2-STROKE
LETTERS

f f   i i   j j   t t   x x   Optional 2-stroke: e e   k k

5mm

*elliptical: shaped like an ellipse—an oval having both ends alike: O

CAPITAL FAMILIES *according to similar letter widths*

CDGOQ · MW · AHKNTUVXYZ · EFILBPRSJ
WIDE   WIDEST   MEDIUM   NARROW

Trace and copy. Fill each line. (Capitals are 1 ½ times the body height of lowercase letters.)

WIDE

C C D D G G O O Q Q

These letters are about as wide as they are tall.

C D G O Q

WIDEST

M M W W

Letters are wider than they are tall.

M W

· SUMERIAN PICTOGRAMS ·

ox   sun   house   (foot) stand go (ideogram)

MEDIUM

A A H H K K

Letters are about 4/5 as wide as they are tall.

A H K

The most ancient system of writing we know of was used by the Sumerians who lived in Mesopotamia before 4,000 BC.

At first, like other cultures, they drew objects simply. Then, as shown above, the picture became a symbol of the object rather than the object itself. These symbols are called pictograms.

Symbols which represent ideas, like "day," "time," "go," "stand," are called ideograms.

N N T T U U

N T U

Do you know we read and write capitals only about 2% of the time?

V V X X Y Y Z Z

V X Y Z

NARROW

E E F F I I or I I L L

NOTE: Stroke 3 lower than 3 on E   I is the narrowest capital

Letters are about 1/2 as wide as they are tall.

E F I I L

B B P P R R or R R S S J J

for rapid writing

B P R S J

CAPITAL PRACTICE

MESOPOTAMIA · 4,000 B.C.

height of caps

M

5mm

CAPITAL LETTERS (CAPS)

In addition to using caps with lowercase letters, plain caps may be used for headings, titles, posters, banners, addresses, abbreviations, certificates, etc.

LARGE CAPS

MEETING · 4 P.M. TODAY · ROOM 2

Cap height line

write P.M. shorter

notice of meeting

M

certificate title

HANDWRITING AWARD

Visualize the height of caps. They are 1 1/2 times the body height.

H

SMALL CAPS

A B C D E F G H I J or J K L M N

Small caps may be written wider than large caps.

A

O P Q R R or R S T U V W X Y & Z

FROM LATIN ET: AND

O

CAP PRACTICE

LARGE CAPS AND SMALL CAPS MAY BE USED SEPARATELY OR TOGETHER

Periods may or may not be used with many abbreviations.

RSVP · P.S. · A.M. P.M.

write a.m. and p.m. in lowercase unless using all caps

R

address

1345 NW CAPITAL

1

State and zip code should be written on the same line on envelopes.

PORTLAND OR 97286

P

MIXED CAPS

THE STORY OF HANDWRITING

by Alfred Fairbank · New York: Watson-Guptil, 1970

T

· CUNEIFORM WRITING ·

About 2500 B.C.

water   dwelling place (house)   mountain

About 1300 B.C.

B   G   P   stylus (writing tool)

(cuneiform - from Latin: cuneus - wedge, forma - shape)

The Sumerians generally wrote on damp clay tablets. Mistakes could be easily smoothed out, but it was difficult to draw curves or circles in the clay. So the scribes began using a wedge-shaped tool of wood, bone or metal which they pressed in the clay.

The use of cuneiform spread to other cultures, among them, Persians, Babylonians and Hittites.

The script finally appeared in one form as a genuine alphabet of 30 symbols in the ancient city of Ugarit in northern Syria.

5mm

body height   1 1/2 times body height

Are your large caps 1 1/2 times the body height of lowercase letters?

G

7

NUMERALS

The word NUMBER stands for an idea—how many objects in a certain group.
The word NUMERAL describes the symbol we use for the number idea.

Just as the first writing happened long after people began speaking, writing numerals to represent numbers came long after people began counting. The earliest numerals known were marks on stones and notches in sticks.

About 3,400 B.C. the Egyptians developed a written number system using hieroglyphics, as shown:

I	II	III	IIII	IIII/II	III/III	IIIII/III	IIII/III	III III/IIII
stroke ~ 1								arch ~ 10

IΩ IIΩ ΩΩ ΩΩ/ΩΩ ΩΩΩΩ ⦾ coiled rope ~ 100 ⦾⦾ ΩΩΩ/III How would we write this? _____

One problem with the Egyptian system and those of the Greeks and the Romans is that none of them had a symbol to represent zero, "not any." In most early systems, people formed numerals by repeating a few basic symbols, then adding their values.

The numerals we use most likely came by way of Arabia from a starting point in India. The Hindus of India had a superior system—a base of ten and symbols for each number from one to nine. This was about 300 B.C. Probably about 900 years later they invented a symbol for zero. However, some sources give credit to Arabia for the zero. Later, these numerals arrived in Europe, first in Spain, and were developed into the system we use and that is used in most parts of the world today.

Beginning of our numerals: O — ≡ ≡ W⊥E ☝ ✶✶

meaning no-thing   2 3 4 5   possibly from 7 stars in Big Dipper constellation   beginnings of 6, 8, & 9 unknown

HINDU-ARABIC NUMERALS
0 0 1 1 2 2 3 3 4 4 5 5 6 6 7 7 8 8 9 9   or 4

Use large numerals when writing with all large caps.

Use small numerals with lowercase and caps and for math.
0 1 2 3 4 5 6 7 8 9

HINDU – ARABIC NUMERALS, A.D. 700

ROMAN NUMERALS
I II III IV V VI VII VIII IX X XI XII
5-1=4 5 5+1=6 10-1=9 10 10+1=11

Roman numerals are written vertically with no slope.

XX L C D M · MCMLXXXVIII
10+10=20 50 100 500 1,000 How would we write this? *

* Write your answer here:_____

5mm

Address 1456 N.W. Lakeview Drive

Note use of small numerals and small caps. Portland OR 97238-1027

Trace & copy lines above.

Write your own address,

and city, state & zip:

Phone no., abbr. date, height or length. (123) 456-7890   3/20/94   5′7″
area code   prefix   number

Money amounts and metric system abbreviations. $15.27   98¢   6 cm   124kg   539km
centimeters   kilograms   kilometers

Time and temperature 8:30 a.m.   12:45 p.m.   74°F   30°C

Usually we write them with small numerals, but write these large. Which do you prefer? ante-meridian - before noon   post-meridian - after noon

Fractions ½ 4⅔ 8¾ 7⅞ 1¹⁵⁄₁₆

Punctuation ' ? ! " " — –
apos-   hyphen dash
trophe

Punctuation adds meaning & expression to written words.

Punctuation and other symbols ( ) ¢ $ or $ * / & &
parentheses   asterisk   slant or slash

CARTOUCHE OF TUTANKHAMUN

A cartouche represents a looped rope indicating the king was ruler of all that the sun encircled.

· EGYPTIAN WRITING ·
3,000 BC – AD 400

Of the three kinds of ancient writing scripts used in Egypt, hieroglyphic is the oldest.* ("hieroglyphic" – sacred engraved writing)

At first, they used only pictograms, then idea pictures – ideograms. Finally they used these to spell words.** Egyptians wrote both horizontally ⇆ and vertically.↓

CARTOUCHE OF CLEOPATRA

TRANSLATION:
K L E O P A T R A   divine female

Above, you can see that all but two symbols were used to spell Cleopatra. The other two symbols are ideograms.

The Egyptians continued to mix their systems rather than using a single system. (At times we also use more than one system: EXIT)

* Only one is mentioned here.
** These then became phonograms.
(A phonogram is a symbol that stands for a single speech sound.)

5mm

G

WRITING PRACTICE

If this book is your first experience writing italic, continue to trace the models before copying.

We use the 26 letters of our alphabet
W
daily in reading and writing, but seldom
d
are we aware of their beginnings.

The body height is now 1mm less (4mm) than on previous pages.

The word ALPHABET
I

²fr¹ ²fi¹
You may connect fr and fi.

comes from the Greek

names of the first two

letters of their alpha-

bet, ALPHA and BETA.

CHECKLIST
___ shape
___ size
___ slope
___ spacing

Some time before 1,300 B.C., the Phoeni-
s
cian alphabet was brought to Greece.

The Greeks added vowels to the alphabet.

· THE PHOENICIAN ALPHABET ·
about 2,000 BC

Many historians feel we can thank the Phoenicians for the beginning of our alphabet. It is thought that their alphabet of 22 letters*was developed from Egyptian hieroglyphs. The Phoenicians used all of their symbols as consonants.

Can you translate this?**

All of those who came in touch with the Phoenicians borrowed their alphabet and changed it to suit their own needs.

SELF-ASSESSMENT: Are you beginning ā ā ḡ ā̧ č š with a horizontal line?

Are you ending b ꞵ with a horizontal line?

4mm

* ⊕ (th) and ꝉ (ts) complete the 22 symbols.
** The Phoenicians wrote from right to left.

G

10

The Greeks also helped determine the direction of our writing. The Phoenicians generally wrote from right to left, and early Greek writing followed this same pattern.

You may cross ft and tt in one stroke. It's faster!

1 LOOK at your writing.

2 PLAN which letters need work. How will you make them look more like the models?

Then the Greeks began writing in both directions as the oxen plowed the fields.* By the 5th century B.C. they had changed to our present way, from left to right.

3 PRACTICE on notebook paper the letters that need more work.

4mm

· GREEK WRITING ·

The Greeks cut letters in stone, scratched letters in clay, wrote on papyrus and on slabs of wood and ivory coated with wax that was stained black. A metal or bone stylus was used to inscribe letters on the wax tablets.

ΑΚΑΔΗΜΙΑ
(ACADEMY)
ΣΧΟΛΗ
(SCHOOL)
ΠΟΙΗΤΗΣ
(POET)

wax tablet *stylus*

Boustrophedon Writing*

SOMEGREEKWRITINGWASWRI
TTENASTHEOXENPLOWEDTHE
LANDMANYLETTERSHADTOB
EREVERSEDASIHAVEDONEHER
EANDTHEGREEKSALSOWROTEL
IKETHISWITHOUTSPACESBET
WEENWORDSANDWITHOUT
ANYPUNCTUATIONMARKS

SELF-ASSESSMENT: Are you leaving about the width of n between words?

to the

G   * boustrophedon: "ox-turning"   11   © 1994 Getty/Dubay

Use basic italic for maps, signs, posters, banners - any time you want something easily read at a distance.

NOTE: In this book, all the writing for student practice and historic notes, such as this map, was written by hand.

Our Writing Heritage

ATLANTIC OCEAN

Romans*

Etruscans

Rome

Greeks*

BLACK SEA

Constantinople

Athens

MEDITERRANEAN SEA

EUPHRATES RIVER

TIGRIS RIVER

Phoenicians

Sumerians

Egyptians

NILE RIVER

KEY
— lowercase and caps - cities
— ALL CAPS - RIVERS
— some cultures that developed written communication
〰〰BODIES OF WATER

*At different times, the Greeks and the Romans influenced much of the area shown on this map.

WRITING LINES: You may reproduce the lines on pages 55-56 for writing practice, or use them underneath as guidelines when writing on plain paper. Choose the writing size which is most comfortable for you—5mm or 4mm.

On this page, the baselines 1-14 are spaced similarly to wide-ruled notebook paper:

The Etruscans acquired the alphabet from the Greeks. In turn, the alphabet was further developed by the Romans.

by
they
the

College ruled:

by
they
the

Today we use all 23 of the Roman letters.**

· THE ETRUSCANS ·
1,000 B.C.-200 B.C.

(The Etruscans apparently came from Asia Minor to Italy and borrowed the Greek alphabet. This tablet shows an early form of the Etruscan alphabet. They remain a people of mystery since no one as yet has been able to translate their writings.)

4mm

** The letters j, u and w were added later.

This is a sketch of an 8th century B.C. Etruscan writing tablet. It is called the MARSILIANA ABECEDARIUM.

Are your letters close together within words? Trace the models for help.

HANDWRITING TIPS

To alleviate pinching your writing tool, tap your finger three times. The way your finger rests on the tool is the way you should hold it as you write. Tap periodically!

•

Note that this is handwriting—not finger or arm writing. Move from the wrist with minimal finger movement. Write an "m" arcade and a "u" arcade for practice:

arch
mmm   mmm   mmm   mmm
counter

uuuu   uuuu   uuuu   uuuu

Write these arcades quickly in a relaxed manner. Practicing the arcade in spare moments—as you wait for an appointment, as you talk on the phone—will help you gain rhythm in your writing.

•

The cursive handwriting many of us learned in school has loops in ascenders and descenders that often cause illegibility.

fill   fill
hill   hill

looped cursive   cursive italic

As you learn cursive italic, begin eliminating the loops in the ascenders and descenders of your own handwriting if you currently use them.

NOTE: Pages 13 and 14 are handwritten.

We read letters from the top— can you read these two words?

AMERICA

VICTORIA

We read the tops of lower-case letters at the waist line area. Italic letters are easily read because they are loop free.

•

Check the interior and exterior counters of families 5 and 6:

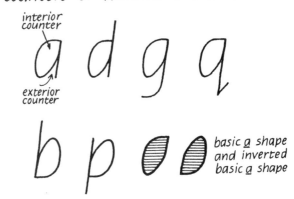

interior counter

a d g q

exterior counter

b p ⬭ ⬭   basic _a_ shape and inverted basic _a_ shape

NOTE: The basic _a_ shape and the inverted basic _a_ shape have identical counters as do the arch: n ⬚ and the inverted arch: ∪ ⬚

Maintaining consistent counters of these letters will help you achieve a harmonious rhythmic hand. Practice the following words:

adage   bundle

pique   pod   NOTE: Invert (rotate) "pod." Are counters consistent?

•

Establish your own waistline when using notebook paper. A consistent body height (_x_ height) is one of the essential characteristics of legibility. (See SIZE GUIDE, p.54)

HANDWRITING TIPS, continued

Look carefully at the letter shapes. It's very easy to say, "I know the shape of <u>A</u> — I've written it all my life." However, you may have overlooked the actual shape of the letter <u>A</u>.

Ways to improve your ability to see shapes: First, look at the negative spaces — the counters of the letters. Draw only the counter shapes and you'll see letters in a new way, for example:

Second, look at letter shapes upside down. It may be exasperating to read, but it is an ideal way to see the shapes of letters.

*ˑuʍop ǝpᴉsdn
buᴉɈᴉɹʍpuɐɥ
uʍo ɹnoʎ Ɉɐ ʞ007*

"In copying signatures, forgers turn the originals upside down to see the exact shapes of the letters more clearly."[1]

•

Let the speed of your writing suit the task, but don't sacrifice legibility for speed. You and others must be able to read it.

•

ONE WAY TO PRACTICE:

1. Trace model.
2. Write letter 3 times.
3. Compare your letter with model.
   Check: a. letter slope
   b. letter width
   c. letter counter
4. Retrace model.
5. Adjust your letter as needed.
6. Rewrite letter alternating with another letter.
7. Evaluate your writing.
8. Close your eyes and write the letter.
   P A T I E N C E

•

If you write a backhand with letters sloping to the left, you can change your letter slope by shifting your paper. There is no need to alter the way you hold your writing tool. It is generally easier to read letters that are vertical or that slope to the right. Whether you are left-handed or righthanded, experiment with paper position.

•

After you complete this book, use italic for all of your handwriting at home and at work. As you journey through this book, begin addressing envelopes for practice. Then start writing letters to friends. Many of us feel we have little time to write letters, but it is a wonderful way to practice your italic and also keep in touch with friends. And once in a-while at the end of a busy day, you may return home and find a reply in your own mailbox.

•

1. Betty Edwards. DRAWING ON THE RIGHT SIDE OF THE BRAIN. Los Angeles: J.P. Tarcher, Inc., 1979, p.51.

PART TWO

Cursive Italic

Cursive Capitals
Transition to Cursive Lowercase
Eight Joins
Writing Practice
Timed Writing
Options
Guidelines

CURSIVE ITALIC CAPITALS

The Roman alphabet is derived from the Phoenician alphabet. The Greeks added vowels to the Phoenician alphabet, which, in turn, evolved from Egyptian hieroglyphs.

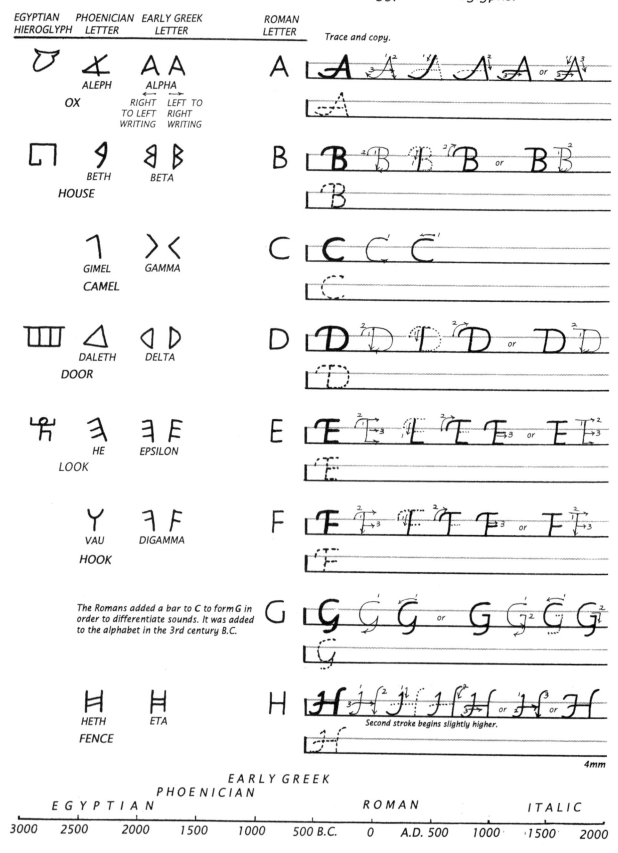

The Romans added a bar to C to form G in order to differentiate sounds. It was added to the alphabet in the 3rd century B.C.

Second stroke begins slightly higher.

4mm

EGYPTIAN HIEROGLYPH	PHOENICIAN LETTER	EARLY GREEK LETTER		ROMAN LETTER	Trace and copy.

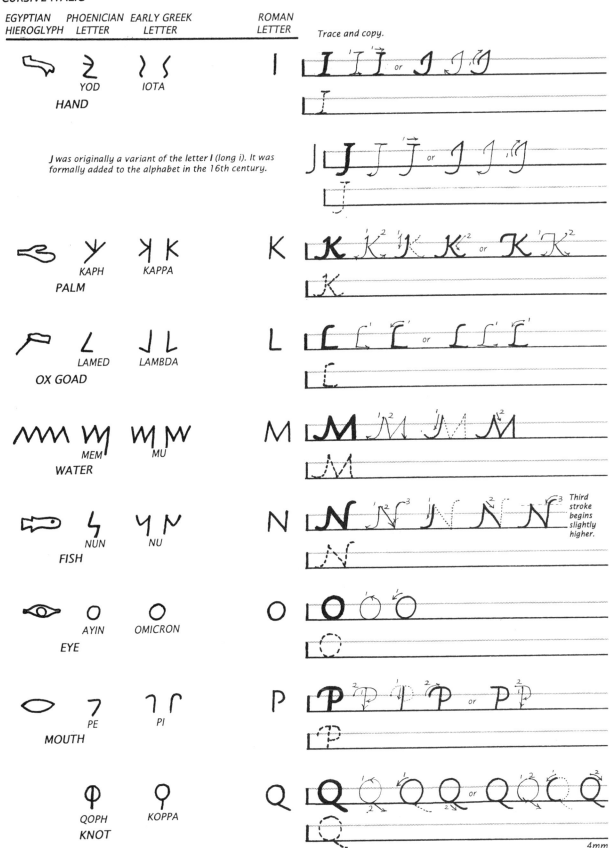

J was originally a variant of the letter I (long i). It was formally added to the alphabet in the 16th century.

HAND — YOD — IOTA

PALM — KAPH — KAPPA

OX GOAD — LAMED — LAMBDA

WATER — MEM — MU

FISH — NUN — NU — *Third stroke begins slightly higher.*

EYE — AYIN — OMICRON

MOUTH — PE — PI

QOPH — KOPPA — KNOT

4mm

Egyptian hieroglyphs are written from top to bottom, usually right to left; also horizontally.

Phoenician letters are written horizontally, right to left, as Hebrew is today.

Early Greek and Roman letters are written in alternating directions, right to left, then left to right, as a field is plowed. See boustrophedon writing on page 11. After c. 500 B.C., the writing direction left to right is established.

EGYPTIAN HIEROGLYPH	PHOENICIAN LETTER	EARLY GREEK LETTER	ROMAN LETTER	

Trace and copy.

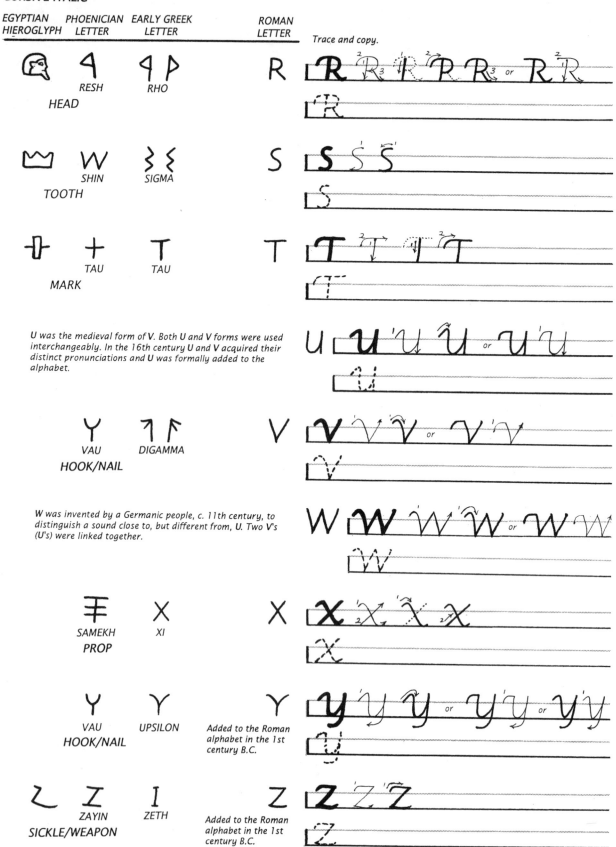

HEAD — RESH — RHO — R

TOOTH — SHIN — SIGMA — S

MARK — TAU — TAU — T

U was the medieval form of V. Both U and V forms were used interchangeably. In the 16th century U and V acquired their distinct pronunciations and U was formally added to the alphabet.

HOOK/NAIL — VAU — DIGAMMA — V

W was invented by a Germanic people, c. 11th century, to distinguish a sound close to, but different from, U. Two V's (U's) were linked together.

PROP — SAMEKH — XI — X

HOOK/NAIL — VAU — UPSILON — Y — Added to the Roman alphabet in the 1st century B.C.

SICKLE/WEAPON — ZAYIN — ZETH — Z — Added to the Roman alphabet in the 1st century B.C.

4mm

The development of the alphabet as shown is based on ANCIENT WRITING AND ITS INFLUENCE by Berthold Louis Ullman (1969 MIT Press).

NOTE: See INSTRUCTION MANUAL, Cursive Italic Capitals, p. 43.

TRANSITION TO CURSIVE LOWERCASE

Serifs are lines added to the main strokes of a letter. Some serifs are slightly rounded and some are sharp. Serifs are used in cursive italic.

soft angle entrance serif — n — soft angle exit serif; sharp angle entrance serif — p

n becomes n · d becomes d · j becomes j (jot)

entrance and exit serifs added · exit serif added · sharp entrance serif

CURSIVE LOWERCASE

a b c d e f g h i j k l m n o p q r s t u v w x y z*

serif (ser'if): a fine line added to a letter

ENTRANCE SERIFS

1 m n r x

Roll into m, n, r, x

2 m n r x

When joining, keep diagonal straight.

3 mn nn nr nx

EXIT SERIFS

4 a d h i (or) i k

Roll out of a, d, h, i, k, l, m, n, u & z

5 a d h i k

6 an dn hn in kn

When joining, serifs are like hands reaching out to join letters.

7 l m n u z

8 l m n u z

When joining, keep diagonal straight.

9 ln mn nn un zn

SHARP ENTRANCE SERIFS

10 j (or) j p v w

Angle into j, p, v & w

11 j p v w

12 nj np

13 nv nw

JOTTED I, J DESCENDER f

jot / or · dot ·

i j i j f

5mm

NOTE: f now descends below baseline.

· ROMAN WRITING ·

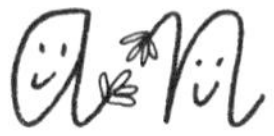

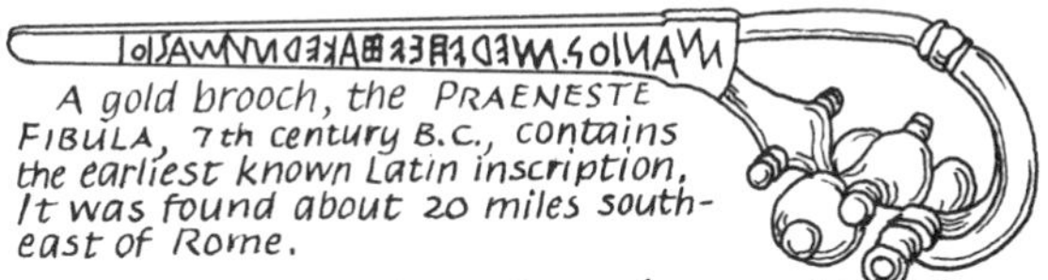

A gold brooch, the PRAENESTE FIBULA, 7th century B.C., contains the earliest known Latin inscription. It was found about 20 miles southeast of Rome.

Early Roman letterforms began with Latin inscriptions in stone and on metal. They also wrote on papyrus, wax tablets, bark & pottery. Their early letters resembled Greek & Etruscan as shown above. Later they became the capital letters we still use today.

* i b c e g o q s t y Remain the same.

BASIC AND CURSIVE CAPITALS WITH CURSIVE LOWERCASE

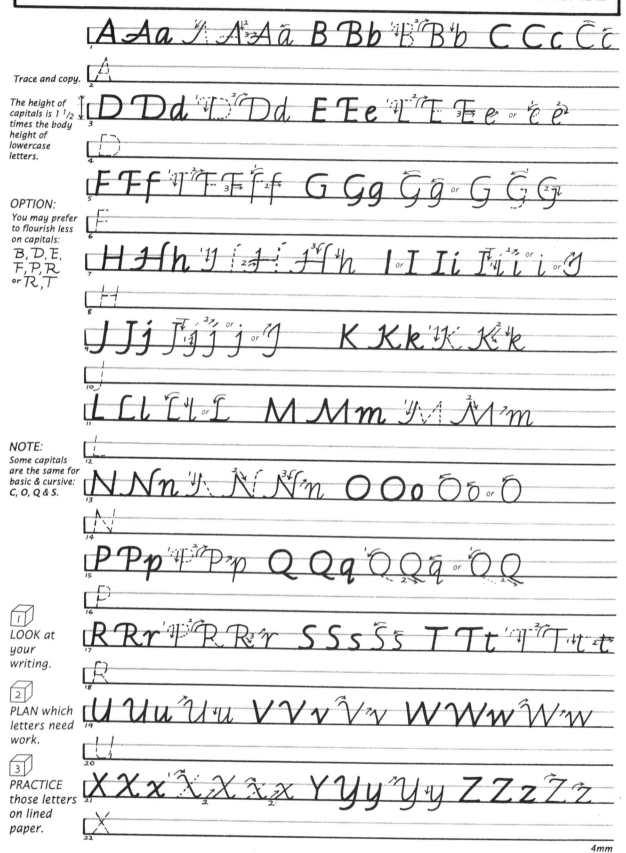

Trace and copy.

The height of capitals is 1 1/2 times the body height of lowercase letters.

OPTION:
You may prefer to flourish less on capitals:
B, D, E, F, P, R or R, T

NOTE:
Some capitals are the same for basic & cursive: C, O, Q & S.

LOOK at your writing.

PLAN which letters need work.

PRACTICE those letters on lined paper.

4mm

OPTION: You may prefer to use basic capitals with cursive italic lowercase:
Ann Bill Carlos Dana Ellen Fay Greg

20

JOIN 1: *an am ar ax* DIAGONAL

Join with a straight diagonal line, then roll over into **n, m, r, x.**

an

an an cn dn en hn in kn ln mn

Trace and copy.

an

nn un zn · Ian Jan Len Ann

nn

am

am em im mm nm um · Sam

am

ar

ar cr dr er ir kr ur

ar

ax

ax ex ix ux · Max

ax

NOTE: For an alternate join into n, m, r, and x see page 23.

Van Dan Kim Pam

V

Cam Tim Sara

C

· PAPYRUS ·

diameter often 20-30 millimeters

rind removed

inner pith sliced into strips

Reeds often grow up to a height of 8 meters.

After the stalks are cut, the thin strips are laid crosswise on a flat surface in a double layer. A cloth is laid over the strips and the papyrus is beaten with a wooden mallet until the strips are matted together.

LOOK at your writing.

Are you joining with a straight diagonal line? *an* (AVOID *an*)

Join 1 is used here. Dotted lines indicate Joins 2-8.

The word "paper" is derived from "papyrus."

The Egyptians, Greeks, and Romans used papyrus as a writing surface.

i

CHECKLIST
____ shape
____ size
____ slope
____ spacing

4mm

NOTE: See INSTRUCTION MANUAL, Cursive Italic Join Descriptions, pp. 46-49.

Assessment, pp. 54-68.

JOIN 2: au ay ai at aj ap av aw
al ah ab ak DIAGONAL SWING UP

Join with a diagonal line blending into a swing-up stroke.

au ay	au ay cu cy du dy eu ey hu hy iu iy

Trace and copy. au

ki ky lu ly mu my nu ny uy zu zy

ki

ai at	ai at ci ct di dt ei et hi ht it ki kt li

ai

It mi mt ni nt ui ut zi · Pat Mimi

it

aj ap	aj ap ej ep ip lp mp np up · Kip

aj

av aw	av aw ev ew iv iw uv uw · Lew Liv

av

OPTION: *You may prefer to round slightly the point of v and the points of w at the baseline.*

av aw ev ew iv iw Lew Liv

aw

al ah	al ah cl ch dl el eh il ih ll ml nl nh

al

ul uh · Sally Philip Emily Anh Vinh

ul

CHECKLIST
___ shape
___ size
___ slope
___ spacing

4mm

22

ab ak | ab ak ck eb ek ib ik lk nk ub uk · Tab

Trace and copy.

[1] **LOOK at your writing.**

Are your joins and letters blending halfway? *att* (AVOID *au*)

Are you joining into **l, h, b, & k** with a single line? *al* (AVOID scoop and loop *al*)

Joins 1-2 are used here. Dotted lines indicate Joins 3-8.

The Latin word for scroll is "volumen" from which comes our word "volume."

[2] **PICK the joins that need work. Compare them with the models. PLAN how to make the joins look more like the models.**

· SCROLL ·

A label (Latin "titulus") is attached to the end for identification.

Some scrolls are more than thirty meters in length.

Both papyrus & parchment are used in scrolls & codices.

· CODEX ·

Sheets are folded for easier storage and transporting.

[3] **PRACTICE those joins on lined paper.**

Parchment, made from the skins of animals, was easier to write on than papyrus and soon became the chief writing material. P

The word "parchment" is from the Latin "pergamena" - from the city Pergamum in Greece. The earliest Greek parchment manuscripts date from the second century B.C.

Sheep, goat, and calf skins are used for parchment.

OPTION: You may prefer to join into **n, m, r & x** with JOIN 2, instead of JOIN 1. *an am ar ax*

an | an en in un · am em im um · Jan Jim

[Options are shown in broken-line boxes.]

an

ar er ir ur · Sara · ax ex ix ux · Max

ax

4mm

JOIN 3: *ao* *as* DIAGONAL START BACK

*Join with a straight diagonal line, then start back into **o** and **s**.*

ao | ao co do eo ho io ko lo mo no uo zo

Trace and copy. | *ao*

as | as cs ds es hs is ks ls ms ns us zs

OPTION: You may prefer to keep the top on **s** when joining:

as

See JOIN 8, page 30.

The top of **s** is left off in this join. See option. | *as*

Leo Julio Luis · L

☐ LOOK | ✎ Are you joining with a straight diagonal? *ao* (AVOID *ao*)

Joins 1-3 are used here. Dotted lines indicate Joins 4-8.

Paper was invented by the Chinese in A.D. 105. P

OPTION: You may prefer to use a 2-stroke **e**. *e* *e*

If so, use JOIN 3. Join into the top of **e**. *ai* *ae*

Follow back out of 2nd stroke. *en* (AVOID *en, en*)

ae | ai ae ce de he ie ke le me ne ue ze

ai ae

en | en eu el eo ee ea · Len Leo Lee Bea

en

Shelley

② PLAN | S

③ PRACTICE | Alex

4mm

· ORIENTAL PAPERMAKING ·

There are eight major steps in the hand papermaking process as practiced since 610 A.D.

Prints from KAMISUKI CHOHOKI, 1798.

Branches cut and bundled.

Outer bark removed.

Wood steamed.

JOIN 4: *ae* DIAGONAL INTO *e*

Join with a diagonal line into *e*.

| *ae* | *ae ce de ee he ie ke le me ne ue ze* |

Trace and copy.

ae

Mae Lee Julie Katie June Sue

M

Alex Theo Zeke Shelley Renée

A

1 LOOK

Is your join into *e* a straight diagonal line? *ae*

Does your join into *e* intersect the letter at the center? center *ae* (AVOID *ae*)

Joins 1–4 are used here. Dotted lines indicate Joins 5–8.

This was written by an ancient Chinese scholar about Ts'ai Lun, a privy councilor to the Royal Court of Ho Ti (89–105 A.D.).

"Ts'ai Lun conceived the idea of making paper from the bark of trees, discarded cloth and hemp well-prepared." "T

2 PLAN

3 PRACTICE

4mm

White bark separated from core and washed.

Bark beaten and beaten still more into pulp.

Mould dipped in vat of pulp and water.

JOIN 5: o͞n t͞n f͞n v͞n w͞n x͞n **HORIZONTAL**
(o͞u o͞o o͞a o͞z o͞t o͞l

These variations are also used with **t, f, v, w** *and* **x.**

Join with a horizontal line into all letters except **f.**

---

on

o͞n om or ox · o͞u oy oi oj op ov ow

Trace and copy. o͞n

o͞o o͞a oc od og oq os o͞z o͞t o͞l oh ob ok.

o͞o

Hoa Thor Joy John Lois Solomon

H

---

tn

t͞n tr t͞u ty ti tw t͞o t͞a ts t͞z t͞l th

The advantage of joining from the crossbar: there is no need to return to cross the **t.**

t͞n.

tt tt Scott Otto Patty Matthew

Double t

tt

OPTION: *You may prefer to join out of the first stroke of* **t** *(from the baseline), then add the crossbar after the word is written.*

tn

tn tn tr tu ty ti tl th to ts te ta

tn

NOTE:
In this book **t** is joined into **e** in this way.

te

te · Pete Kate Nate

te

OPTION: *You may prefer to join out of* **t** *into* **e** *with a horizontal join.*

te

See page 27 for other options.

---

fn

f͞n fr f͞u fy fi· fj fo fa fs · ft ft or ft ft· fl

fn

ff ff ff· Jeff Cliff Clifton

A list is suggested before **e** *after* **f.**

ff

4mm

OPTION: *You may prefer to join out of* **f** *into* **e** *with a horizontal join.*

fe

| vn | vn vr · vu vy vi · vo · va vs · vt vl · Aviva |

Trace and copy. vn

| wn | wn wr · wu wy wi · wo · wa ws · wt wl |

wn

wh wk · Lewis Edwin Newton

wn

| xn | xn · xu · xy xi · xo · xa x.s · xt · xl |

xn

Alexis Maxine · A

1 LOOK ✏ Are you joining with a straight, horizontal line? on (AVOID on)

Joins 1-5 are used here. Dotted lines indicate Joins 6-8.

Hand papermaking processes today use plant fibers or rag pulp.

H

2 PLAN

3 PRACTICE

NOTE: Join into e out of o, v, w, and x with a diagonal join.   OPTION: te fe

| oe | oe ve we xe · Joe Eve Gwen Axel |

oe

OPTION: You may prefer to lift before e after o, t, f, v, w, and x.

| oe | oe te fe ve we xe · Joe Eve Peter |
or Peter (see p.26)

oe

OPTION: You may prefer to use a 2-stroke e after o, t, f, v, w, and x.

| oe | oe te fe ve we xe · Joe Eve Peter |

oe

4mm

JOIN 6: rn ru ro ra re **DIAGONAL OUT OF r**

Join with a short diagonal line into all letters except f.

| rn | rn rm rr · Arne Carmen Larry |

Trace and copy. rn

| ru | ru ry ri rt rv rl rh rb rk · Art |

ru

| ro ra | ro · ra rc rd rs · Arturo Sara Cars |

ro

| re | re · Karen Greta |

OPTION: If you prefer a 2-stroke e, join into the top of e. re² Karen

re

rc re²

LOOK at your writing.

Are you joining out of r just below the waistline?
Are you bending the top of r at the waistline?

waistline
rn (AVOID m rn may look like m or vn)

Joins 1-6 are used here. Dotted lines indicate Joins 7-8.

Hand papermaking mills use this process today.

NOTE: The join out of r needs more practice than any other join. Legibility depends on it being done well.

· WESTERN PAPERMAKING ·

Deckle
frame fits tightly over the mould

Mould
Woven brass wires are attached to frame

Vat of pulp & water

Cotton or linen rags are beaten in water to form the pulp. The mould and the deckle are immersed in the vat of pulp. A thin layer of pulp is gathered on the mould.

SIDE VIEW pulp deckle mould

The deckle is removed and the mould with the layer of pulp is turned over and rolled onto a piece of felt

pulp placed on felt

After being pressed, dried, and sized, a piece of paper is ready to write on.

OPTION: You may prefer to point the top of r to aid legibility. rn

| rn | rn ru ro re · Sara |

rn

OPTION: You may prefer to lift after r to aid legibility.

| ru | ru ro ra re · Karen · ru |

If you prefer to lift after r, keep letters close together.

4mm

JOIN 7: *sn bn pn* HORIZONTAL TO DIAGONAL

Join with a horizontal line blending into a diagonal line into all letters except **f**.

---

sn

sn sm sr *or* sn sm sr · su sy si st sp sv

Trace and copy. sm

sv sl sh sb sk · so ss *or* ss · se · sa sc sd sg

sw

Jessie José Justin J

bn

bn br *or* bn br · bu by bi bt bl bb · bo bs

bn

be · ba bc bd bg · Pablo Bobby Deborah

be

pn

pn pr *or* pn pr · pu py pi pt pp pl ph · po

pn

ps *or* ps · pe · pa pc pd pg · Hope Joseph

ps

LOOK at your writing.

Are you following back out of *s*, *b*, & *p*? *sr br pr* (AVOID *br pr*)

Joins 1-7 are used here. Dotted lines indicate Join 8.

Wood is the basic raw material from which most machine made paper is manufactured. W

Some machine-made papers are made with 100% wood fiber, some 100% cotton rag, and some are mixtures.

4mm

OPTION: You may prefer to lift after **b** and **p**. If so, be sure the next letter follows closely. *br pr bo po*

JOIN 8: *aa ac ad ag aq as* **DIAGONAL TO HORIZONTAL**

Join with a diagonal line blending into the horizontal beginning strokes of *a, c, d, g, q,* and *s.*

---

aa ad | aa ad ca ea ed da dd ha ia id ka

Trace and copy. | aa

ia ld ma na nd ua ud za ·Shalonda

ia

ag aq | ag aq eg eq ig iq ng ug uq · Quang

ag

ac | ac cc ec ic uc · Vic Alice Michael

ac

as | as cs ds es hs is ks ls ms ns us zs

as

Joins 7 & 8 | sa sc ss · ba · pa ps · Lissa Barbara

sa

LOOK at your writing.

Are your a, c, d, g, q, and s flat on top? *aa* (AVOID *aa* or *aa*)

All joins are used here.

PLAN how to make the joins look more like the models.

CHECKLIST
____ shape
____ size
____ slope
____ spacing

PRACTICE the joins which need more work.

Our word "pen" is from the Latin word for feather—"penna."

· PENS ·

The first pens were cut from reeds.

Later, flight feathers of geese or swans were used.

Quills were the primary pen used for writing on parchment and paper until the 19th century.

4mm

LIFTS: *af az · ga ja qu ya* (NO JOINS)

Lift writing tool before f and z and after g, j, q, and y.

af | Olaf Jeffrey Alfredo Alfreda

Trace and copy.

az | Alonzo Lizzie Kazuaki Elizabeth

Lift before z from the baseline.

ga ja | Inga Bridget Helge Elijah Sonja

qu ya | Jacqueline Joyce Beryl Lloyd Sylvia

Joins are natural spacers. When letters in a word are not joined, be sure they are close together. af az ga ja qu ya

OPTION: You may prefer to join out of **g, y, q,** and **y.** go jo qu yo

Speed may alter the shape of descenders so they are straighter, longer or more curved.
yg gyj

We read letters from the top (see page 13). For the sake of legibility do not add loops to ascenders. Addition of loops to descenders does not hamper legibility if adequate space is left between lines of writing.

REVIEW | 1 an am ar ax (an am ar ax) ·

Options in parentheses.

2 au ay ai at aj ap av aw al ah ab ak · 3 ao as

(aea) · 4 ae · 5 on tn (tn) fn vn wn xn ·

6 rn (rn) · 7 sn bn pn · 8 aa ac ad ag aq as

A quick brown fox jumps over the lazy dog.

4mm

WRITING PRACTICE

SENATVS·PO
IMP·CAESARI·I
TRAIANO·AV(
MAXIMOTRIB

The Trajan Inscription · Roman Forum
112-113 A.D. *Cast by Edward Catich (small portion shown)*
From THE ROMAN LETTER by James Hayes

The actual height of S (top left) is 4 ⁵/₈".

* Note the exception to the horizontal join out of t. The join from t to one-stroke e is from the baseline.

te

Other options:
te te te
See pages 26-27.

CHECKLIST
___ shape
___ size
___ slope
___ spacing

The Roman inscriptional letters* serve as the models for our capitals.

They were written* with a brush, then incised in the stone and painted.

Square Capitals were derived from the large inscriptional letters.

They were written with a reed pen on parchment and used as a bookhand from the first to the fifth centuries.

4mm

SQUARE CAPITALS

ABCDEFGHIKLMNOPQRSTVXYZ

After Virgil manuscript - 4th century   *The 23 letters of the Roman alphabet.*

RUSTIC CAPITALS

ABCDEFGHIKLMNOPQRSTUXYZ

After Virgil manuscript 4th-5th century.

Rustics were written with a reed pen on papyrus and parchment.

The flowing, narrow letters of Rustics show the influence of speed and the need to conserve materials. This script was used mainly for special editions of poetry. T

The name Uncial comes from St. Jerome—meaning "inch-high".

We see in Uncial the beginning of our lowercase letters:

λ → a, a
δ → d
e → e
h → h
m → m
q → q

Uncial writing was used primarily for copies of the Bible. The curving forms show the desire to make letters with the fewest possible strokes. Uncial was used from the third century to the tenth century. u

1 LOOK

2 PLAN

3 PRACTICE

4mm

UNCIAL ABCDEFGHIKLMNOPQRSTUXYZ

After Gospels of St. Gall—5th-6th century.

abcdefghiklmnopqrfstuxyy&z
(long s)

CAROLINGIAN

In the 9th century, an increased interest in culture led to the copying of the Latin classics. This led to the advancement of writing.

The Carolingian script was used for copying large quantities of Latin manuscripts. In use from 800 to 1200, these letters have lengthened ascenders and descenders.

CHECKLIST
___ shape
___ size
___ slope
___ spacing

At its best, Gothic is beautiful but hard to read.

The Gothic script is the bookhand of the late Middle Ages. Its angular letters show the need to save space.

uite often large letters appear at the beginning of paragraphs.

This Q is from a manuscript written by Claricia, a nun c. 1200. She represents herself as the tail of the Q. (From WOMEN ARTISTS by K. Peterson and J. Wilson.)

4mm

abcdefghijklmnopqrstuxyz GOTHIC

Around the 13th century, a faint slash was added to i to aid legibility.

ROTUNDA abcdefghiklmnopqrstuvxyz
(round Gothic)

15TH CENTURY BOOKHAND
(HUMANIST BOOKHAND)

abcdefghiklmnopqrſstuxy&z·jvw
(long s)

The scholars collected classical texts—many written in Carolingian. Their Gothic hand (Rotunda) was influenced by the elegant Carolingian to create 15th century bookhand.

A clear, legible bookhand was
developed during the Renaissance
by Italian scholar-scribes in the
fourteenth & fifteenth centuries.
It is the basis of many typefaces.

The transition from bookhand to cursive is:
1) round to elliptical forms

O to O

2) vertical to slightly sloped

on to on

3) unjoined to joined.

iu to iu

Italic, a cursive form of this bookhand, flourished for two hundred
years as the basic script for business
and correspondence. Today it con-
tinues as a practical handwriting.

1 LOOK
2 PLAN
3 PRACTICE

ITALIC

Anonymous scribe 1490 (The Houghton Library, Harvard University, Department of Printing and Graphic Arts.) Reproduced by permission.

altior ordo ſacerdotalis · Stephanus qq:
papa ſecundus Romanum imperium
in perſonam magnifici caroli á Grecis
transtulit in Germanos · Alius itē Ro

4mm

Seguita lo essempio delle' lre'che'pono ligarsi con tutte'le'sue sequenti, in tal mo= do Cioe'

aa ab ac ad ae' af ag ah ai ak al am an

ao ap aq ar as af at au ax ay az

Il medesmo farai con d i k l m n u.

Le ligature' poi de' c f s ʃ t sonno le'infra= scritte

ɛt, fa ff fi fm fn fo fr fu fy, ʃt st

ʃf ʃʃ ß ʃt, ta te' ti tm tn to tg tr tt tu tx ty

Con le restanti littere'de'lo Alphabeto,che' sono, b e'g h o p q r x y z z non si deue' ligar mai lra alcuna sequente'

The first instruction manual of the italic script was LA OPERINA by Arrighi, printed in Rome in 1522.

ITALIC

LA OPERINA, Ludovico degli Arrighi, Italy, 1522
THE FIRST WRITING BOOK by John Howard Benson
(Yale University Press, 1954). Reproduced by permission.

Letters above are angular as they were cut and printed from woodblocks.

In Italy, italic served as a personal hand for many, including Raphael, Michelangelo, and Cellini.

Writing on pages 36–37 offers practice using the baseline only— similar to notebook paper.

NOTE: The two-stroke e is used in this paragraph. (See OPTION page 24.)

In England this script became known as the "italique hande." Italic was the hand of courtiers, secretaries, and royalty.

CHECKLIST
_____ shape
_____ size
_____ slope
_____ spacing

ROUND HAND
THE UNIVERSAL PENMAN
by George Bickham
(Dover Publications, Inc., New York)
LETTERING: MODES OF WRITING IN
WESTERN EUROPE FROM ANTIQUITY TO
THE END OF THE 18TH CENTURY by
Hermann Degering (Taplinger/Pentalic,
1978). Reproduced by permission.

abbcddefoghhiijkkllllmnnoppqrsfstuvnxyz.
ABCDEFGHIJKLMMM.
NNOP2RSTUVWXXYYZ.

During the 17th to 19th centuries, round hand was written with a flexible nib on paper and with an engravers' burin on copperplate.

Round hand was the result of the addition of ornate flourishes, loops on ascenders & descenders, more pen lifts, and an extreme slope of 38°.

The looped cursive or "commercial cursive" in use today is patterned after round hand. The loops, extreme slope, and forced joins make looped cursive often illegible when written fast.

Italic handwriting, with its roots in the Renaissance, provides a handsome, graceful script for today. Both basic italic and cursive italic serve well as a practical, legible handwriting.

"Cursive" comes from the Latin "currere" —to run.

Cursive italic maintains its legibility when written quickly.

Italic is a loop free, clean-cut script for the computer age.

NOTE:
To increase writing speed, do Timed Writing exercise on page 38.

You will develop your own unique personal hand. See OPTIONS page 39.

Handwriting is a lifelong skill, and good handwriting is a lifelong joy!

1. LOOK
2. PLAN
3. PRACTICE

ℭ Write cursive italic with an edged pen.

4mm

See EDGED PEN ITALIC pages 42-49.

Begin by writing the following sentence on another sheet of paper as a warm-up for the timed writing. If you prefer, substitute another pangram or sentence.

A quick brown fox jumps over the lazy dog.

1. TIME LENGTH: 1 MINUTE Write the sentence at your most comfortable speed. If you finish before the time is up, begin the sentence again.

_____

_____

Count the number of words written and write the number in Box 1.

Box 1

2. TIME LENGTH: 1 MINUTE Write the sentence a little faster. Try to add 1 or 2 more words to your total.

_____

_____

Write the number of words written in Box 2.

Box 2

3. TIME LENGTH: 1 MINUTE Write the sentence as fast as you can. Maintain legibility.

_____

_____

Write the number of words written in Box 3.

Box 3

4. TIME LENGTH: 1 MINUTE Write the sentence at a comfortable speed.

_____

_____

Write number of words written in Box 4.

Box 4

The goal is to increase the number of words written per minute. Aim for an increase in the total of Box 4 over Box 1. Speed can be increased while maintaining legibility. Repeat process often.

EYES CLOSED *Using the same sentence, do this exercise as a follow-up to timed writing. Begin with a non-lined sheet of paper. Close your eyes. Picture in your mind's eye the shape of each letter as you write. Take all the time you need. You may be amazed how well you can write with your eyes closed.*

© 1994 Getty/Dubay, *Italic Handwriting Series*
PSU, Continuing Education Press
P.O. Box 1394, Portland, OR 97207

> **OPTIONS** A personal handwriting style is created by variations of shape, size, slope, spacing, and speed.

SHAPE Italic is based on an elliptical shape which may be standard, expanded, or compressed.

Standard   *a quick brown fox jumps over the lazy dog*

Expanded   *a quick brown fox jumps over the*

Compressed   *a quick brown fox jumps over the lazy dog*

SIZE Each person has a comfortable letter size.

4mm   3mm   2½mm

a quick brown fox jumps over the lazy dog

SLOPE Writing slope may vary from 0° to 15°. Standard slope is 5°. Whichever slope is preferred, be consistent. See *Slope Guidelines*, page 40.

0°   *a quick brown fox jumps over the lazy dog*

5°
(standard)   *a quick brown fox jumps over the lazy dog*

10°   *a quick brown fox jumps over the lazy dog*

15°   *a quick brown fox jumps over the lazy dog*

SPACING The spacing between letters in a word and between words may be standard, expanded, or compressed. See *Spacing Guidelines*, page 40.

Standard
spacing   *a quick brown fox jumps over the lazy dog*

Expanded
spacing   *a quick brown fox jumps over the*

Compressed
spacing   *a quick brown fox jumps over the lazy dog*

SPEED Let the speed of writing fit the need, maintaining legibility. Notice how speed affects shape, size, slope, and spacing.

Moderate
speed   *a quick brown fox jumps over the lazy dog*

Rapid
speed   *a quick brown fox jumps over the lazy*

As you progress, italic handwriting becomes personal and unique. Whichever combinations of options are used, the goal is even shape, even size, even slope, and even spacing.

SLOPE GUIDELINES

The *Italic Handwriting Series* is written with a 5° slope. Both basic italic and cursive italic are written with the same 5° slope—there is no need to change.

OPTIONS: The *Italic Handwriting Series* offers a choice of slope—from a vertical of 0° to a slope of 15°. *Slope Guidelines* are shown on page 54. Whichever slope is preferred, the goal is to maintain a consistent slope. The choice range is:

0° 1° 2° 3° 4° 5° 6° 7° 8° 9° 10° 11° 12° 13° 14° 15°

NOTE: As we write we all vary slightly from our chosen slope. We are not machines! An overall, even, balanced writing is our goal. See OPTIONS, page 39.

ASSESSMENT: *LOOK at your writing. Are you writing with an even slope? Are you using a 5° slope? What is your choice of slope?*
If the slope is uneven, use the following exercise to find your natural slope:

1. Write a word.
2. Check the consistency of the slope by drawing slope lines through the center of each letter (line up with the downstroke or axis of each letter).

3. Choose the slope which appears most often, as in Example A or choose the slope in the middle range, as in Example B.
4. Then draw parallel lines next to the slope you have chosen.
5. Use the parallel lines as your slope guide.

	EXAMPLE A	EXAMPLE B
1. Write word.	slope	slope
2. Draw slope lines over letters	slope	slope
3. Pick one slope	slope	slope
4. Draw parallel lines	/////	|||||
5. Write over slope lines	slope	slope

PLAN how to write with an even slope.
Use a slope guide under the writing paper. If the slope is more than 15° or a backhand is used, changing the paper position often helps. (Generally, a backhand slope is difficult to read; a slight backhand slope is acceptable.)

As you progress, the goal is to write with a consistent slope of your choice (between 0° and 15°).

SPACING GUIDELINES

There are two aspects of spacing: the space between letters within a word and the space between words in a sentence.

Space between letters:
The letters within a word are close together. In basic italic, there are three rules of spacing:

1. Two downstrokes are the farthest apart.

2. A downstroke and a curve are a little closer.

3. Two curves are the closest, almost touching.

Spaces 1, 2, & 3 equal in area   hill   home   pod
1   2   3

In cursive italic, joins are natural spacers. When lifts occur between letters (before **f** and **z**; after **g, j, q,** and **y**), keep letters close together to avoid gaps.

Space between words:
Leave the width of **n** between words.

Use the width of an n between words.

OPTIONS: Standard spacing is used in this book. Expanded and compressed spacing are other choices.

standard   standard
expanded   expand
compressed   compressed

In the space below write with your most comfortable spacing. Aim for even, balanced writing.

· abcdefghijklmnopqrstuvwxyz ·

PART THREE

Edged Pen Italic

Italic with the Edged Pen
Basic Italic
Cursive Italic
Chancery Cursive
Pangrams
Personal Correspondence
Greeting Card and Booklet

· abcdefghijklmnopqrstuvwxyz ·

ITALIC HANDWRITING WITH THE EDGED PEN
writing tools / inks / papers / how to sit / pen hold & pen angle

WRITING WITH AN EDGED PEN will help make your handwriting look handsome, beautiful, official! You'll need to spend time developing the correct pen hold and using the letters — but you'll probably find it will be well worth the cost of pen, ink & paper. You can bring yourself and others pleasure through your writing.

WRITING TOOLS

Many edged tools are available — fiber and felt-tip pens, cartridge ink pens, fountain pens and dip nibs. (A nib is a pen tip.) You can also cut your own pens from ice cream sticks, tongue depressors, paint stir sticks, cattail stalks, green garden stakes, bamboo reeds, etc. A few are shown below:

The left-handed person may find left oblique nibs helpful, but the square cut nibs can be used.

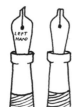 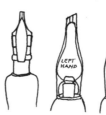 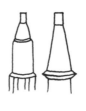 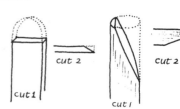

FOUNTAIN PENS   PENHOLDERS WITH DIP NIBS   FIBER-TIP PENS   TONGUE DEPRESSOR   CATTAIL STALK
(for large letters)

INKS

Be sure to use fountain pen ink in fountain pens. If you're using a dip nib, use ink that is <u>not</u> waterproof (unless you need your writing waterproofed). Waterproof inks generally contain shellac and tend to clog dip pens — and ruin fountain pens. You can learn to write with any kind of ink. Be sure to stir the bottle before using and replace the cap after each use. Black and many colors are available. Try mixing two colors of the same type and brand to create your own color.

PAPERS

For practice, white typing paper or a bond paper will usually provide a suitable writing surface. Avoid onionskin and easy-to-erase paper. The best way to select paper is to write on a sample piece to see if it takes ink well and does not feather. Colored papers can add interest to your writing — try colored butcher paper for large signs. Construction paper is usually too rough and porous. Most papers are machine made, but a few are made by hand. *See pp. 36, 37 and 40 for more information about papermaking.*

Both letters 1 & 2 were written → with the same pen on different paper.

$^1 n$ $^2 n$

feathering

HOW TO SIT

Rest your forearms on the writing surface, feet flat on the floor and keep your back comfortably straight as you lean slightly forward.

It is easier to get the entire edge of your pen nib on the surface of your paper if you write on a slanted board.

A   B

If you are left-handed, try either paper position A, B, or somewhere in between. If you write from above the line, hold paper similar to C or D.

C   D

If you are right-handed, use paper position C for rapid everyday writing. For careful (formal) work, hold paper as in D.

PENHOLD & ANGLE

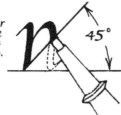

Hold your pen with thumb and index finger resting it on the middle finger. Rest the shaft near the large knuckle.

45°

Pen edge lies at 45° angle to the writing line. This allows pen edge to form the correct thicks and thins as you write lowercase letters.

BASIC ITALIC

GUIDE-LINES

The body height of italic lowercase letters is generally four or five pen widths regardless of the size of the pen. The pen is held horizontally to mark off the pen widths to measure the distance between guidelines.

Guidelines:

BASIC ITALIC   CURSIVE ITALIC

ascender line
waistline
baseline
descender line

45°   ↑body ↓height

ascender → cap   ascender → cap

aghfP · aghfP

←descender   ←descender

In this book the ascender and descender lines are not shown since ascenders and descenders have been shortened. The shortened letters allow you to write faster. If you are carefully writing out a poem, quotation, etc., you may wish to extend your ascenders and descenders to 4 or 5 pen widths each.

Caps are always written 1½ times body height of lowercase.

extra fine

Calligraphy – beautiful writing.

extended ascenders and descenders

BASIC STROKES

Don't shift pen or arm – keep pen edge at a constant 45° pen edge angle to the baseline.

45° + + + + ∧∧∧ /// \\\ ⋈⋈⋈ mm uuu

Trace & copy.

BASIC ITALIC

ii jj ll · kk or kk vv ww xx zz ·

See pages 2–5 for lowercase families.

hh mm nn rr · uu yy · bb pp

To write the size shown on lines 1–13, use a fine nib. Dip nibs are also available in this size.

aa dd gg qq · e or e o @ cc ss · ff tt

See page 6 for capital families.

CDGOQ · M W · A H K N T U V X Y Z

overlap at A & B

Flatten pen edge angle between 15°–30° for caps.* (But stay at 45° for rapid writing.)

E F L B P R R S J Y · 0 1 2 3 4 5 6 7 8 9 9 · . , ? ! " "

Alphabet Sentence

A quick brown fox jumps over the lazy dog.

or k

* To flatten pen edge angle to 15°–30°, keep the <u>same</u> pen hold, but:
LEFT-HANDED · move elbow away from your body to flatten pen edge angle.
RIGHT-HANDED · move right elbow closer to your body.

CURSIVE ITALIC

BASIC STROKES

Trace & copy each line of writing.

45° serif serif

waistline
baseline

SERIF ALPHABET

a b c d e f g h i j k l m n o p q r s t u v w x y z

ENTRANCE SERIFS

Roll into m, n, r, x.

mmm   nnnn   rrrr   xxxx or *x*

EXIT SERIFS

Roll out of a, d, h, i, k, l, m, n, u, z.

aaaa   ddd   hhh   iii   kk or *k*

lll   mm   nnn   uuu   zzz

SHARP ENTRANCE SERIFS

Angle up into j, p, v, w.

jjjj   ppp   vvvv   wwww

NO CHANGE

These letters remain the same as the basic italic letterforms, except the f now descends below the baseline.

bbb   ccc   eee or *eee   ggg   ooo*

qqq   sss   ttt   yyy   fff

JOINS

Lowercase letters are joined together for cursive handwriting.

JOIN 1

Diagonal - roll over into m, n, r, and x.

an · am an ar ax or *ax*

JOIN 2

Diagonal - swing up into b, h, i, j, k, l, p, t, u, v, w, and y.

au · ab ah ai aj ak al ap at au av

aw ay · OPTION: *an am ar ax*

4mm

JOIN 3

Diagonal - start back into o and s.

ao · ao as · OPTION: ae

JOIN 4

Diagonal into e.

ae · ae ee ie ue te

JOIN 5

Horizontal out of f, o, t, v, w, and x.

on · fn on tn vn wn xn

JOIN 6

Diagonal out of r.

rn · ra re ri ro ru rz

JOIN 7

Horizontal to diagonal out of b, p, and s.

sn · bn pn sn

JOIN 8

Diagonal into horizontal top of a, c, d, g, q, and s.

aa · aa ac ad ag aq as

LIFTS

Lift before f and z. Lift after g, j, q, & y.

af az · gn jn qu yn

EXERCISE

For more practice with joins, see pages 21-31. Use lines on page 55 or 56 as a lined sheet under your writing paper.

ana bnb cnc dnd ene fnf gng hnh ini

jnj knk lnl mnm nnn ono pnp qnq rnr

sns tnt unu vnv wnw xnx yny & znz

SENTENCE PRACTICE

Thomas Carlyle 1795-1881 Scottish essayist & historian.

Certainly the art of writing is the most

miraculous of all things man has devised.

~: Examples for training the Hand :~

A·cc abc dice'f c g hik lmnopq pg

orsstuxxyz Et st sf sf ss sti ww

No Glory comes at the start, but at the end.

Thus is born honor, true &

perfect:

Why enter the field of battle, & then flee?

Ille Idem & Vicetinus Scribebat Rome.

Translation by John Howard Benson of LA OPERINA by Ludovico degli Arrighi, Rome, 1522. THE FIRST WRITING BOOK by John Howard Benson (Yale University Press, 1955.) Reproduced by permission.

Writing with an edged pen at a 45° angle creates a thin line for the diagonal join — a pleasing contrast.

an

For a thinner horizontal line, flatten the pen edge angle slightly for the crossbar of f and t and also for Join 5 (similar to pen edge angle for capitals, page 43).

4mm

CURSIVE CAPITALS

A B C D E F G H I or II J or JJ K

L M N O P Q R R S T U or U V

W X Y or Y or Y or Y Z · Use these caps with lowercase only. Don't write entire words with these caps.

Flatten pen edge angle between 15° and 30° for carefully written caps. Stay at 45° for rapid writing.

Lowercase joins: abcdefghijklmnopqrstuvwxyz

CAPITAL PRACTICE

Principal rivers of the world written with a "fine" nib.

Amazon Brazos Columbia Danube

Euphrates Fraser Ganges Huang Ho

OPTION: You may prefer a 2-stroke e with the edged pen,

ae ae

with a flourish out of e.

Indus Juruá Kolyma Loire or Loire   two-stroke e

Mississippi Nile Orinoco Paraná

Quarai Rhine Snake Tigrus Ural

OPTION: You may prefer to begin i, u, and y with a serif.

i, u, y

Volga White Xingu Yukon Zambezi

4mm

SENTENCE PRACTICE

Written with an "extra fine" nib.

A true source of human happiness lies in taking
a genuine interest in all the details of daily life
and elevating them by art. WILLIAM MORRIS

3mm

G

46

CHANCERY CURSIVE ·
In the 15th and 16th centuries, the chancery cursive hand developed. The chancery was the office where official documents were kept, and chancery cursive was the official handwriting for these records.

A flourish is a flowing curve.

Beginning serifs on i, u, y:

FLOURISHED ASCENDERS & DESCENDERS

bb dd hh kk ll ff gg jj pp ii uu yy

ASCENDERS: With a dip pen, move slightly to the right before moving left.

CHANCERY LOWERCASE

abcdefghijklmnopqrstuvwxyz

NOTE: Ascenders are taller and descenders are longer.

CHANCERY CAPITALS

AA BB CC DD EE FF GG

Trace & write:

For carefully written caps, flatten pen edge angle to 15°-30°. Stay at 45° for rapid writing.

GG HH II or II JJ or JJ KK LL

Be sure this is a sharp angle on H, K, M, N, U, V, W.

MM NN OO PP QQ QQ RR

Keep horizontals straight except for slight curve at A & B.

There are many different choices of Chancery caps.

SS TT UU VV WW XY YZ

SENTENCE PRACTICE

The first italic instruction book was written by Ludovico degli Arrighi (Vincentino). It is printed from wood blocks, therefore, it is thought the letters appear more angular than the actual handwriting of that time.

Arrighi's La Operina
the first italic instruc
tion manual, was pub
lished in Rome in 1522.

4mm

Remember, your handwriting is a personal statement. For careful (formal) writing, you may choose to use fewer joins.

~: Exempli per firmar la Mano :~

A·eoabcodieefeg hiklmnopqpg orsstuxxyz. ff st ssffßstuww

No e' Gloria il principio, ma il seguire. De' qui nasce' l'honor uero. & perfci to: Che' vale' in campo intrare', et poi fuggire'?

Ille' Idem. L. Vice'tinus Scribebat Rome.

FROM LA OPERINA by Ludovico degli Arrighi, Rome, 1522. THE FIRST WRITING BOOK by John Howard Benson (Yale University Press, 1955.) Reproduced by permission.

PANGRAMS

Each sentence contains all 26 letters of the alphabet.

BASIC ITALIC

Quick wafting zephyrs vex bold Jim.

NOTE:
2-stroke k on
line 1; 1-stroke
k on line 3.

LOOK at
your
writing.

Picking just six quinces, new farmhand proves strong but lazy.

PLAN which
letters need
work.

PRACTICE
those letters
on lined
paper.

A large fawn jumped quickly over white zinc boxes.

CURSIVE ITALIC

Fred specialized in the job of making very quaint wax trays.

NOTE:
2-stroke e in
"very."

NOTE:
Lift after w in
"vowed."

Six crazy kings vowed to abolish my quite pitiful jousts.

Jack amazed a few girls and boys by dropping the antique onyx vase.

4mm

PANGRAMS
continued

Many big jackdaws quickly zipped

over the fox pen.

M

Five or six big jet planes zoomed

quickly by the new tower.

CHECKLIST
____ shape
____ size
____ slope
____ spacing

F

CHANCERY CURSIVE

Waltz, nymph, for quick jigs vex Bud.

W

NOTE:
2-stroke e in
"vex'd."

Frowzy things plumb vex'd Jack Q.

F

I quickly explained that many big

jobs involve few hazards.

J

UNJOINED CHANCERY

A quick brown fox jumps over the lazy dog.

A

For further
practice use the
Dubay/Getty
calligraphy
manual:
*Italic Letters:
Calligraphy &
Handwriting,*
Continuing
Education Press
1992

Quickly pack the box with five dozen

modern jugs.

Q

4mm

One of the anticipations of each week-day is checking the mail. How grand it is when we receive a handwritten message from a friend. You can bring joy into the lives of others with a cheery note or letter — and you can practice your handwriting at the same time. Surprise a friend with your words!

letters. Write on! • Dear Reader, Not all letters have to be written on

WRITE LETTERS ON LONG STRIPS

Use them for standard sizes sheets of paper. Sometimes print shops will sell or give you endcuts.

Sometimes messages can be written at random. Not all of your correspondence has to be designed the same.

Dan

Put a surprise in the envelope by designing your own format.

Dear Rosalie   March 20, 1994

To answer your question, yes, many elementary schools throughout the United States are now using italic handwriting — HOORAY!
After teaching elementary school students for a number of years, I know the frustration many students experience changing from print script to commercial cursive handwriting. It also seems that many high school students & adults abandon their cursive hand and return to a modified print script because at least it's legible. Besides, we are a "please print" nation since many people can't read other people's cursive handwriting.
By writing italic from kindergarten on, no change in letterforms is experienced — the student begins with basic italic, then adds cursive italic joins in second or third grade. With italic, the student learns 52 letterforms (26 lowercase, 26 capitals) for a lifetime of hand-writing legibility and enjoyment. With print script and commer-cial cursive, 104 letterforms must be mastered.
Hopefully, more and more schools will be adopting italic as a total handwriting program.
We hope to visit you again one of these years — but until then, just remember post cards are always in good taste!

Happy writing,
Barbara

There's more to it than just wiggling your fingers and out come the letters

Dear Dan,
I under-stand you're learning italic handwriting. TERRIFIC! One of the best ways to exercise your new skill is by writing notes and letters to your friends. You might write a short quote on the left with a wider pen, then the text at the right as I have written here. Love, Barbara 15 · IX · 94

HOWARD GLASSER

quoted with permission of Howard Glasser

See Pop-up card designs INSTRUCTION MANUAL, page 85.

ENVELOPES

Design your own envelope by using a commercial envelope for a pattern. Cut your envelopes from plain paper, gift wrap paper, or large magazine covers. For the last two papers, use a self-sticking label for the address & attach the stamp with adhesive.

Margaret
420 JFK BLVD
PHILADELPHIA
PA · 17614

2763 N. Beach Drive
ROGER BAIN
Catalina · CA · 98761

MARTIN · MAR Beverly TIN · MARTIN · MARTIN
572 POLK AVENUE
MIAMI · FL · 12345

Chuck
Vernon
Chuck
Vernon
Chuck
Vernon
CHUCK VERNON
Chuck 25 Murray, Atlanta, GA 47561
Vernon
Chuck
Vernon
Chuck

HAPPY BIRTHDAY HAPPY BIRTHDAY
Arlene Robs
723 S. Elm
Boise, ID 11136
HAPPY BIRTHDAY

Note: The state and zip code should be written on the same line

GREETING CARD

To make a greeting card for a business size envelope, 10.5 cm x 24 cm (4 $^1/_8$ x 8 $^1/_2$ in), you will need:
· scissors · yarn or thread, 90 cm (35 $^1/_2$ in) · needle · ruler · paper clips
· 1 sheet typing paper (or similar) cut to 19 cm x 22 cm (7 $^1/_2$ in x 8 $^3/_4$ in) for inside of card
· 1 sheet colored paper (heavier than typing) cut to 20 cm x 23 cm (8 x 9 in) for cover of card

a. Fold both sheets lengthwise and crease.

b. Insert typing paper inside cover.

c. Paper clip sheets together.

d. On the inside, make a center dot A and one on either side at equal distances from the center, BC.

e. Push needle through the 3 dots ABC to establish stitching holes.

f. Stitch sheets together as follows:

　1) From outside cover, pass needle through center hole A, leaving 15 cm (6 in) for tying.

　2) From inside, pass needle through hole B to outside of card.

　3) From outside, skip over A, pass needle through third hole C to inside.

　4) From inside, pass needle through center hole A to outside.

　5) Tie knot over the long stitch. Cut ends to 4 or 5 cm (approximately 1 $^1/_2$ or 2 in); or instead of cutting ends, tie in bow as shown.

g. Complete cover and inside message before or after stitching.

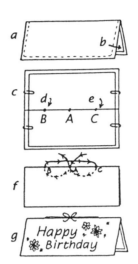

SMALL BOOK

Add a few more inside pages as in illustration b. You may fold all of your sheets either direction:

two stitches　　　four stitches

The four-stitch bookbinding is a bit stronger—tighten each stitch as you go along. Decorate your cover with a drawing, potato print, etc.

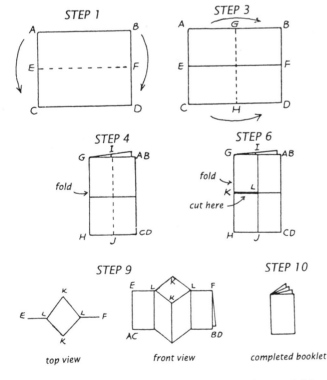

top view　　front view　　completed booklet

NOTE: In illustrations above, dotted line indicates fold that occurs within the given step. Solid lines within rectangle indicate folds previously established.

See INSTRUCTION MANUAL:
Envelope Instructions, p. 81, and Envelope Pattern (A2 size) p. 108.

SURPRISE BOOKLET

Use as a small booklet, greeting card, or personal note.

Materials: sheet of light or medium weight paper and scissors.

A 28 cm x 43 cm (11" x 17") sheet will give a finished size of 10.8 cm x 14 cm (4 $^1/_4$" x 5 $^1/_2$"). This size will fit an A-2 envelope.

1. Fold AB to CD to establish EF.

2. Open back to original size.

3. Fold AC to BD to establish GH.

4. Fold GH to AC/BD to establish IJ.

5. Open to previous fold (GH/AB/CD).

6. With scissors, cut KL by cutting halfway between GH, stopping at fold IJ.

7. Open to original size ABCD.

8. Refold AB to CD as in #1.

9. Grasp E/AC with left hand and F/BD with right hand, then push hands together, establishing three leaves on one side and one on the other.

10. Fold remaining leaf over the other three pages. Two leaves have folds at the top and two on the fore edge of the booklet.

beginning of letter　　middle of letter　　end of letter

GLOSSARY

ASCENDER ▪ The part of a letter that extends above the waistline.

ARCH ▪ The part of a letter resembling an arch, such as the round portion of "n."

BASELINE ▪ The line on which letters "sit," bottom line of body height (sometimes called the writing line).

BASIC ITALIC ▪ A form of unjoined writing using italic letters without entrance or exit serifs.

BODY HEIGHT ▪ The distance between baseline and waistline (sometimes called "x" height).

BRANCHING LINE ▪ An imaginary line halfway between the baseline and waistline.

CALLIGRAPHY ▪ Beautiful or elegant writing, also the art of producing such writing. The letters are generally unjoined and often written with the edged tool. Italic calligraphy is one type of formal hand lettering or writing.

CAPITAL LETTER ▪ A letter in the series **A,B,C**, rather than **a,b,c** (sometimes called upper-case, large letters, or caps).

COUNTER ▪ Partially or fully enclosed space within a letter.

CROSSBAR ▪ A horizontal line, second stroke of **f** and **t**.

CURSIVE ITALIC ▪ A form of joined writing using italic letters with entrance and exit serifs. [Medieval Latin SCRIPTA CURSIVA - "Flowing script" - from Latin CURSUS, past participle of CURRERE - "to run."] Four characteristics of a cursive hand are elliptical forms, slight slope, fluent (mostly one-stroke letters), and joined letters.

DESCENDER ▪ The part of a letter that extends below the baseline.

DIAGONAL ▪ A line from lower left to upper right (as used in joins and letter shapes) or a line from upper left to lower right (as used in letter shapes).

DOWNSTROKE ▪ A line from top to bottom following letter slope angle.

ELLIPTICAL SHAPE ▪ A line following a compressed circular shape or elongated circle (as in *o*).

HORIZONTAL ▪ A line extending from left to right, parallel to baseline and waistline.

INTERSPACE ▪ An area between letters within words.

INVERTED ARCH ▪ The part of a letter resembling an upside-down arch such as "u."

ITALIC ▪ A script originating in Italy in the late 15th and early 16th centuries. It is characterized by slightly sloped, elliptical, fluent and often joined letterforms.

ITALIC HANDWRITING ▪ A system of writing for everyday use incorporating both an unjoined form of writing (basic italic) and a cursive form of writing (cursive italic).

JOT ▪ A short diagonal above i and j in place of a dot.

LETTER DIMENSIONS
  SHAPE ▪ The correct form of a capital or lower-case letter.
  SIZE ▪ The height and width of a letter.
  SLOPE ▪ The slant of a letter.
  SPACING ▪ The space between letters in words and space between words in a sentence.
  SPEED ▪ The rate of writing.

LOWERCASE LETTER ▪ A letter in the series **a, b, c**, rather than **A, B, C** (sometimes called small letters). [From the printer's practice of keeping the small letters in lower type cases or drawers.]

PEN EDGE ANGLE ▪ The angle of the edge of the pen nib in relation to the baseline.

SANS SERIF ▪ Without serifs, without any additions to the letter, as in basic italic.

SERIF ▪ An entrance or exit stroke of a letter.

STROKE ▪ Any straight or curved written line.

UPPERCASE ▪ See CAPITAL LETTER. [From the printer's practice of keeping the large letters in the upper type cases or drawers.]

WAISTLINE ▪ The top line of the body height.

BIBLIOGRAPHY

Anderson, Donald M. *Calligraphy: The Art of Written Forms.* New York: Dover Publications, 1992.

Anderson, Donna. "The Italic's Answer to Illegibility." *Vancouver Sun* (B.C.), February 21, 1976.

Benson, John Howard. *The First Writing Book, An English Translation & Fascimile Text of Arrighi's* Operina, *The First Manual of the Chancery Hand.* New Haven: Yale University Press, 1955.

Catich, Edward M., *The Origin of the Serif.* Davenport, Iowa: The Catfish Press, St. Ambrose College, 1993. Originally published 1968.

Dubay, Inga and Barbara Getty. *Italic Letters: Calligraphy and Handwriting.* Portland, Oregon: Continuing Education Press, Portland State University, 1992.

Edwards, Betty. *Drawing On the Right Side of the Brain.* Los Angeles: J.P.Tarcher, Inc., 1979.

Encyclopaedia Britannica s.v. "Numerals." Chigago: Encyclopaedia Britannica, Inc., 1993. 8: 826–27.

Fairbank, Alfred. *A Handwriting Manual.* New York: Watson-Guptill Publications, 1975.

Getty, Barbara, & Inga Dubay. *Italic Handwriting Series (Books A, B, C, D, E, F, G and Instruction Manual).* 3rd. ed. Portland, Oregon: Continuing Education Press, Portland State University, 1994.

————— *Write Now: A Complete Self-Teaching Program for Better Handwriting.* Portland, Oregon: Continuing Education Press, Portland State University, 1991.

Groff, Patrick J. "Preference for Handwriting Styles by Big Business." *Elementary English,* 41 (December, 1964): 863-64, 868.

Hayes, James. *The Roman Letter.* Chicago: The Lakeside Press. n.d.

Jarman, Christopher J. *The Development of Handwriting Skills,* Great Britain: Basil Blackwell,1979.

————— *Fun with Pens.* New York: Taplinger Publishing Co., 1979.

Lehman, Charles L., with contributing authors Donald Cowles and Gertrude Hildreth. *Handwriting Models for Schools.* Portland, Oregon: The Alcuin Press, 1976.

Petersen, Karen & J. J. Wilson. *Women Artists: Recognition and Reappraisal from the Early Middle Ages to the Twentieth Century.* New York: New York University Press/Harper & Row, 1976.

Reynolds, Lloyd J. *Italic Calligraphy and Handwriting.* New York: Pentalic, 1969.

Temple, Charles A., Ruth G. Nathan, and Nancy A. Burris. *The Beginnings of Writing.* Boston: Allyn and Bacon, Inc., 1982.

Ullman, B.L. *Ancient Writing and its Influence.* New York: Cooper Square Publishers, Inc. 1963.

Wallace, Don. "Sending The Right Message," *Success Magazine,* 62 (April 1989).

————— • —————

G

Italic Handwriting Series
Continuing Education Press
P.O. Box 1394
Portland, OR 97207

5mm lines

Italic Handwriting Series
Continuing Education Press
P.O. Box 1394
Portland, OR 97207

G

Italic Handwriting Series
Continuing Education Press
P.O. Box 1394
Portland, OR 97207